Beloved Savior

© 2001 Simon Dewey; Altus Fine Art, LLC

All rights reserved. No part of this book may be reproduced in any form or by any means without permission in writing from the publisher, Deseret Book Company, P. O. Box 30178, Salt Lake City, Utah 84130. This work is not an official publication of The Church of Jesus Christ of Latter-day Saints. The views expressed herein are the responsibility of the author and do not necessarily represent the position of the Church or of Deseret Book Company.

Eagle Gate is a registered trademark of Deseret Book Company.

Visit us at www.deseretbook.com

ISBN 1-57345-964-X

Printed in the United States of America   42316-6816

Inland Press, Menomonee Falls, WI

10 9 8 7 6 5 4 3 2 1

Beloved Savior

IMAGES FROM THE LIFE OF CHRIST

ARTWORK BY SIMON DEWEY

EAGLE
GATE

SALT LAKE CITY, UTAH

Contents

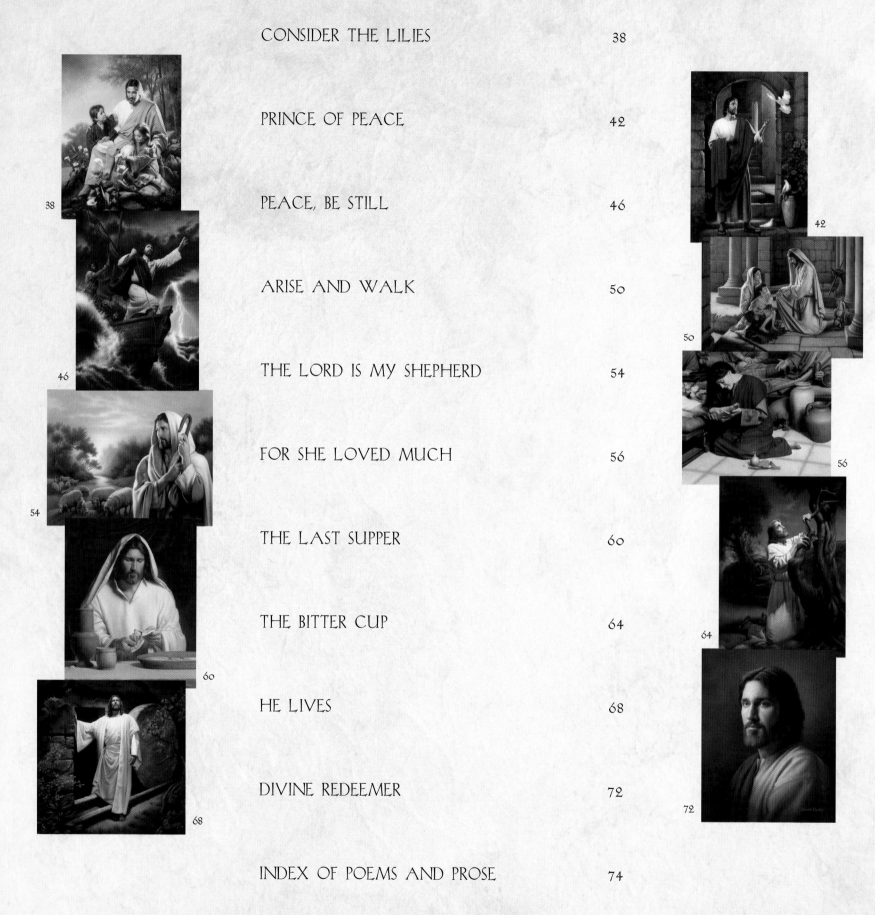

Preface

No life has been more celebrated in the arts than that of our Savior Jesus Christ. Be it through prose, painting, sculpture, or song, our Savior and his atoning sacrifice have been the focus, even the lifelong passion, of innumerable artists. Images of our Savior in either sculpture or painting have been particularly powerful influences in the Christian world. During times when many believers could neither read nor write, beautiful works portraying the Savior provided the masses with inspiring representations of his life and mission, giving both illuminating beginnings and abiding reminders of faith. The universal language of the painter was, in those times, the people's scripture.

Through today's technology we enjoy the accumulation of these timeless works as well as works from contemporary artists. While technology has brought new tools to the artist's palette, the challenge of today's painter of Christ remains the same. How does one create images of such heavenly things with limited earthly materials? What means can be used in the finite to express the infinite? How does the artist express his overwhelming feelings in a way that is worthy of his subject of worship? To endeavor to paint the face of the Son of God is an awesome and, in some ways, audacious task. But whether it is the simple line drawing of a child or the exquisite rendition of a master painter, if the heart is right, the result is the same. The work becomes an honest expression of love and gratitude, a pure offering of worship.

Artist Minerva Tiechert said, "A true artist cannot paint anything he cannot feel." This book is the result of Simon Dewey's feelings for the subject most dear and sacred to him. Those who know Simon know that his work is more than an application of talent and discipline. It is an expression of who he is.

It is our hope that these beautiful images—representations of centuries past—combined with divine scripture and prose will inspire hearts and souls as they reside in the minds of young and old alike. As sweet memories of happy times past, may these images rest in your consciousness—willing to come forward when they are most needed. It is in this spirit that Simon Dewey adds his work to the countless efforts of those artists who have used a brush and canvas in praise of our Lord and Master, our beloved Savior, Jesus Christ.

—The Publisher

WHAT CAN I GIVE HIM

CHRISTINA ROSETTI

❧ ❧ ❧

What can I give Him,

Poor as I am?

If I were a shepherd

I would bring a lamb.

If I were a Wise Man

I would do my part,

Yet what can I give him?

Give my heart.

Simon Dewey

For Unto Us a Child Is Born

For unto you is born this day in the city of David a Saviour, which is Christ the Lord. And this shall be a sign unto you, ye shall find the babe wrapped in swaddling clothes, lying in a manger.

—LUKE 2:11–12

His Name Shall Be Called Wonderful

FOR UNTO US A CHILD IS BORN,

UNTO US A SON IS GIVEN: AND THE

GOVERNMENT SHALL BE UPON HIS

SHOULDER: AND HIS NAME SHALL BE

CALLED WONDERFUL, COUNSELLOR,

THE MIGHTY GOD, THE EVERLASTING

FATHER, THE PRINCE OF PEACE.

—ISAIAH 9:6

THERE'S A SONG IN THE AIR!

JOSIAH GILBERT HOLLAND

There's a song in the air!
 There's a star in the sky!
  There's a mother's deep prayer
  And a baby's low cry!
  And the star rains its fire while the beautiful sing,
  For the manger of Bethlehem cradles a King!

  There's a tumult of joy
   O'er the wonderful birth,
For the Virgin's sweet boy
Is the Lord of the earth.
Ay! the star rains its fire while the beautiful sing,
For the manger of Bethlehem cradles a King!

In the light of that star
Lie the ages impearled;
And that song from afar
Has swept over the world.
Every hearth is aflame, and the beautiful sing,
In the homes of the nations that Jesus is King!

We rejoice in the light,
And we echo the song
That comes down thro' the night
From the heavenly throng.
Ay! we shout to the lovely evangel they bring,
And we greet in His cradle, our Saviour and King!

LIGHT OF THE WORLD

AUTHOR UNKNOWN

Light of the world so clear and bright,
Enter our homes this Christmas night;
Relight our souls so tenderly.
That we may grow to be like Thee.

Picture the humble surroundings in which the most precious infant in all history lay asleep on the hay.

Mary—the loving and attentive mother—and Joseph—the worthy guardian—watch over the babe with awe and wonder, likely feeling the way all new parents have throughout the ages. And yet, they know something else.

For this child, their child, will be "The mighty God, The everlasting Father, The Prince of Peace" (Isaiah 9:6). But to them on that holy night, he and his blessed name are simply—Wonderful.

Let us rejoice as we reflect on this sacred event that was Christ's birth. And as we remember the magnitude of God's love in allowing his Son to leave his side and enter a world of sorrows, let us in our hearts, in our homes, and throughout our lives call him Wonderful.

—Simon Dewey

With God, nothing shall be impossible.
This Mary knew even as she stood
before the angel Gabriel and took in his
wondrous message. All that transpired
between that sobering point and the
moment Mary held the infant Jesus in
her fragile arms must have been a sure
witness of God's omnipotence. Mary
kept all these things and pondered them
in her heart and doubtless looked to the
future. In the magnificence of her situation, she must have been bemused that
this defenseless babe, to whom she had
given life, with all the attributes and
needs of any infant, would some day
surrender his life in order that she might
live. She must have wondered how this
child would one day be called the Son of
the Highest, inheriting the throne of
David, ruling over the house of Jacob
forever, Lord of a kingdom without end.

And, just like Mary's newborn son,
every child that comes to this earth
possesses divine origins and therefore
infinite potential. Perhaps that is why
the human heart rarely fails to be moved
by the sight of a tiny baby.

—Simon Dewey

My Son, My Savior

❖

BUT MARY KEPT

ALL THESE THINGS,

AND PONDERED

THEM IN HER HEART.

—LUKE 2:19

Simon Dewey

HIS MOTHER KEPT
ALL THESE SAYINGS
IN HER HEART

WILLIAM CULLEN BRYANT

As o'er the cradle of her Son
The blessed Mary hung,
And chanted to the Anointed One
The psalms that David sung,

What joy her bosom must have known,
As, with a sweet surprise,
She marked the boundless love that shone
Within his infant eyes.

But deeper was her joy to hear,
Even in his ripening youth,
And treasure up, from year to year,
His words of grace and truth.

Oh, may we keep his words like her
In all their life and power;
And to the law of love refer
The acts of every hour.

THE NAME OF MOTHER

GEORGE GRIFFITH FETHER

The holiest words my tongue can frame,

The noblest thoughts my soul can claim,

Unworthy are to praise the name

More precious than all other.

An infant, when her love first came,

A man, I find it still the same,

Reverently I breathe her name,

The blessed name of mother.

The scriptures say very little about Jesus the boy, but we know that he grew in much the same way that all children do. By the time he was twelve, however, he had become advanced for his age, both spiritually and mentally. Still, there must have been treasured moments between Mary and her first-born son in which teaching and learning took place on both sides.

This depiction shows Mary taking time at the end of a busy day to pray and give thanks to a beloved Father in Heaven with their Son at her knees. The lamp casts a warm light on the evening scene and symbolizes the light of truth and example that emanates from the Savior.

If we, like Mary, train up our children in the ways of the Lord, we can receive blessings and truth that will guide us and our children throughout their lives.

—Simon Dewey

In Favor with God

AND JESUS INCREASED IN WISDOM

AND STATURE, AND IN FAVOUR

WITH GOD AND MAN.

—LUKE 2:52

Simon Dewey

CHILD'S EVENING HYMN

SABINE BARING-GOULD (ADAPTED)

Now the day is over,
    Night is drawing nigh,
Shadows of the evening
    Steal across the sky.

Now the darkness gathers,
    Stars begin to peep,
Birds and beasts and flowers
    Soon will be asleep.

Jesus, give the weary
    Calm and sweet repose,
With thy tenderest blessing
    May our eyelids close.

Grant to little children
    Visions bright of thee,
Guard the sailors tossing
    On the deep blue sea.

Comfort every sufferer
    Watching late in pain;
Those who plan some evil
    From their sin restrain.

Through the long night-watches
    May thy angels keep
Loving watch about me,
    Guarding as I sleep.

When the morning wakens,
    Then may I arise
Pure and fresh and sinless
    In thy holy eyes.

Your birth of the

Pure and fresh and sinless

Little is known about the honorable Joseph, the just and faithful carpenter who was entrusted from on high to foster the Only Begotten Son of God. We do know that with a valiant heart he did as he was bidden by the angel in a dream: he took Mary as his wife and nurtured her and her Son with loving-kindness.

There must have been opportunities at the end of the working day when tools were pushed aside and Jesus took time to learn his Father's business. Perhaps he did so with Joseph at his side. Certainly, in the process of tutoring the growing Jesus, we can imagine that Joseph would have been learning as much as he was teaching.

For us, Joseph is a remarkable example of parental guidance and love. From him we see that there is much we can learn about humility and meekness from our little ones.

—Simon Dewey

Growing in Wisdom

AND THE CHILD GREW, AND WAXED

STRONG IN SPIRIT, FILLED WITH WISDOM:

AND THE GRACE OF GOD WAS UPON HIM.

—LUKE 2:40

Simon Dewey

O SON OF MAN,
THOU MADEST KNOWN

MILTON S. LITTLEFIELD

O Son of Man, Thou madest known,
Through quiet work in shop and home,
The sacredness of common things,
The chance of life that each day brings.

O Workman true, may we fulfill,
In daily life the Father's will;
In duty's call, Thy call we hear
To fuller life through work sincere.

Thou Master Workman, grant us grace
The challenge of our tasks to face;
By loyal scorn of second best,
By effort true, to meet each test.

And thus we pray in deed and word,
Thy kingdom come on earth, O Lord;
In work that gives effect to prayer
Thy purpose for Thy world we share.

THE HIDDEN YEARS AT NAZARETH

ALLEN EASTMAN CROSS

The hidden years at Nazareth,
How beautiful they seem,
Like fountains flowing in the dark
Or waters in a dream!
Like waters under Syrian stars
Reflecting lights above,
Repeating in their silent depths
The wonder of God's love!

The hidden years at Nazareth!
How marvelous they lie,
As open to the smile of God
As to the Syrian sky!
As open to the heart of man
As to the genial sun,
With dreams of high adventuring,
And deeds of kindness done!

The hidden years at Nazareth!
How radiant they rise,
With life and death in balance laid
Before a lad's clear eyes!
O soul of youth, forever choose
Forgetting fate or fear,
To live the truth, or die with God,
Who stands beside thee here!

Beside Still Waters

❧

HE MAKETH ME TO LIE DOWN

IN GREEN PASTURES: HE LEADETH

ME BESIDE THE STILL WATERS.

HE RESTORETH MY SOUL:

HE LEADETH ME IN THE PATHS OF

RIGHTEOUSNESS FOR HIS NAME'S SAKE.

PSALM 23:2–3

Simon Dewey

Fishers of Men

AND JESUS SAID

UNTO THEM,

COME YE AFTER ME,

AND I WILL MAKE

YOU TO BECOME

FISHERS OF MEN.

—MARK 1:17

Simon Dewey

23

The call to Simon Peter and Andrew to follow the Savior as fishers of men echoes down through the centuries and applies to us all. Those two faithful brothers left their nets immediately to begin their missions.

We, however, need not turn aside from our mortal responsibilities. We can be missionaries in our own homes, in the workplace, and at play. Our Lord bids us to follow him, meaning that we need to look to his example, emulate his attributes, and live his teachings. In so doing, people will be drawn inexorably to us as those in Israel were drawn to the Son of Man. Our light can be a beacon to those seeking the truth, and with the Spirit as our guide we can help bring souls unto Christ.

—Simon Dewey

ye after me

THOU DIDST TEACH
THE THRONGING PEOPLE

JEMIMA T. LUKE

Thou didst teach the thronging people
By blue Galilee;
    Speak to us, Thy erring children;
        Teach us purity.

        Thou whose touch could heal the leper,
        Make the blind to see;
            Touch our hearts and turn from sinning,
            Into purity.

        Thou whose word could still the tempest,
        Calm the raging sea,
            Hush the storm of human passion,
        Give us purity.

Thou didst sinless meet the tempter.
Grant, O Christ, that we
May o'ercome the bent to evil,
By thy purity.

Light and Truth

SEARCH THE SCRIPTURES; FOR IN THEM YE THINK YE HAVE
ETERNAL LIFE: AND THEY ARE THEY WHICH TESTIFY OF ME.

—JOHN 5:39

As Jesus traveled about Galilee, teaching the gospel and preaching repentance, he one day returned to his own country, to Nazareth. And on the Sabbath, he went to the synagogue to speak and teach.

"And there was delivered unto him the book of the prophet Esaias. And when he had opened the book, he found the place where it was written,

"The Spirit of the Lord is upon me, because he hath anointed me to preach the gospel to the poor; he hath sent me to heal the brokenhearted, to preach deliverance to the captives, and recovering of sight to the blind, to set at liberty them that are bruised, . . .

"And he closed the book, and he gave it again to the minister, and sat down. And the eyes of all them that were in the synagogue were fastened on him.

"And he began to say unto them, This day is this scripture fulfilled in your ears" (Luke 4:17–18, 20–21).

For those who thought of Jesus as only Joseph's son, this declaration was hard to take. In anger, they rose up and thrust the Lord out of the city.

May those of us who believe his words—who know him to be the Savior of the world—never be guilty of thrusting him out of our lives. As he kindly offers us his light and truth, may we be uplifted and edified—worthy to be called his friends.

—Simon Dewey

Lord, speak to me

LORD, SPEAK TO ME, THAT I MAY SPEAK

FRANCES R. HAVERGAL

Lord, speak to me, that I may speak
In living echoes of Thy tone;
As Thou hast sought, so let me seek
Thy erring children lost and lone.

O teach me, Lord, that I may teach
The precious things Thou dost impart;
And wing my words, that they may reach
The hidden depths of many a heart.

O fill me with Thy fullness, Lord,
Until my very heart o'erflow
In kindling thought and glowing word,
Thy love to tell, Thy praise to show.

O use me, Lord, use even me,
Just as Thou wilt, and when and where;
Until Thy blessed face I see,
Thy rest, Thy joy, Thy glory share.

JESUS, MIGHTY KING IN ZION

JOHN FELLOWS

❦

Jesus, mighty King in Zion,

Thou alone our guide shall be.

Thy commission we rely on;

We will follow none but thee.

As an emblem of thy passion

And thy vict'ry o'er the grave,

We, who know thy great salvation,

Are baptized beneath the wave.

Fearless of the world's despising,

We the ancient path pursue,

Buried with the Lord and rising

To a life divinely new.

Simon Dewey

Living Water

WHOSOEVER DRINKETH OF THE

WATER THAT I SHALL GIVE

HIM SHALL NEVER THIRST; BUT

THE WATER THAT I SHALL

GIVE HIM SHALL BE IN HIM A

WELL OF WATER SPRINGING

UP INTO EVERLASTING LIFE.

—JOHN 4:14

It was at Jacob's well, in the presence of a lowly Samaritan woman, that Jesus chose to declare his Messiahship in one of the most tender and profound teaching moments in the New Testament. He could have delivered his message to a large multitude of learned and favored individuals. Yet he took time to meet quietly with this woman, who was in much need of the sweet forgiveness and hope that only one like unto God could have offered her.

We do not know the duration of their discussion, but we can imagine that as light and comfort filled the woman's heart, there was a well of water springing up within her unto everlasting life. As we worship the Father in spirit and truth and study and pray, living water can flood through our souls, and we will thirst no more.

—Simon Dewey

HIS GRACE IS GREAT ENOUGH

ANNIE JOHNSON FLINT

❧ ❧ ❧

His grace is great enough to meet the great things —
The crashing waves that overwhelm the soul,
The roaring winds that leave us stunned and breathless,
The sudden storms beyond our life's control.

His grace is great enough to meet the small things —
The little pin-prick troubles that annoy,
The insect worries, buzzing and persistent,
The squeaking wheels that grate upon our joy.

THE KING OF LOVE

HENRY W. BAKER

The King of love my Shepherd is,
    Whose goodness faileth never;
I nothing lack if I am His,
    And He is mine forever.

Where streams of living water flow
    My ransomed soul He leadeth,
And where the verdant pastures grow
    With food celestial feedeth.

Perverse and foolish oft I strayed,
    But yet in love He sought me,
And on His shoulder gently laid,
    And home rejoicing brought me.

In death's dark vale I fear no ill,
    With Thee, dear Lord, beside me;
Thy rod and staff my comfort still,
    Thy life before to guide me.

Thou spread'st a table in my sight;
    Thy suff'ring grace bestoweth;
And O what transport of delight
    From Thy pure chalice floweth.

And so, through all the length of day,
    Thy goodness faileth never;
Good Shepherd, may I sing Thy praise
    Within Thy house forever

Simon Dewey

Touch of Faith

❖

AND AS MANY AS TOUCHED WERE MADE PERFECTLY WHOLE.

—MATTHEW 14:36

There is such great power in the story of the woman who, after bearing the burden of ill health for twelve years, knew that only the slightest contact with the Son of God would cure her. We know from the scriptures that later, after word was spread abroad concerning this miracle, that as many as touched the Savior's robe were healed. In a figurative sense we can reach out in our moments of trial and pain and touch our Master, whose power to heal is as present today as it was when he walked among men.

—Simon Dewey

STRONG SON OF GOD
FROM *IN MEMORIAM*

ALFRED, LORD TENNYSON

Strong Son of God, immortal Love,

    Whom we, that have not seen thy face,

    By faith, and faith alone, embrace,

Believing where we cannot prove;

        ❊   ❊   ❊

We have but faith: we cannot know,

    For knowledge is of things we see;

    And yet we trust it comes from thee,

A beam in darkness: let it grow.

LET NOTHING DISTURB THEE

HENRY WADSWORTH LONGFELLOW

❖

Let nothing disturb thee,

Nothing affright thee;

All things are passing;

God never changeth:

Patient endurance

Attaineth to all things;

Who God possesseth

In nothing is wanting;

Alone God sufficeth.

As Jesus prepared his disciples to go out and teach the people of the earth, he told them: "Take no thought for your life, what ye shall eat, or what ye shall drink; nor yet for your body, what ye shall put on" (Matthew 6:25). In simple faith, the disciples were told to turn to the Lord for all their needs.

In a similar matter, little children turn to loving parents to supply all their needs. And we too must become like little children, having faith that a loving Father will readily provide. If we seek for the kingdom of God first, all these things will be added unto us. If we, with childlike faith, center our lives on Christ and live according to his word, we can be assured we will prosper.

—Simon Dewey

Consider the Lilies

SUFFER THE LITTLE CHILDREN

TO COME UNTO ME, AND FORBID

THEM NOT: FOR OF SUCH IS

THE KINGDOM OF GOD.

—MARK 10:14

Simon Dewey

OUT IN THE FIELDS WITH GOD

ELIZABETH BARRETT BROWNING

❧

The little cares that fretted me,

I lost them yesterday

Among the fields above the sea,

Among the winds at play;

Among the lowing of the herds,

The rustling of the trees,

Among the singing of the birds,

The humming of the bees.

The foolish fears of what may happen

I cast them all away

Among the clover-scented grass,

Among the new-mown hay;

Among the husking of the corn

Where drowsy poppies nod,

Where ill thoughts die and good are born,

Out in the fields with God.

I THINK WHEN I READ THAT SWEET STORY

JEMIMA T. LUKE

I think when I read that sweet story of old,

When Jesus was here among men,

How he called little children as lambs to his fold;

I should like to have been with him then.

I wish that his hands had been placed on my head,

That his arms had been thrown around me,

That I might have seen his kind look when he said,

"Let the little ones come unto me."

Yet still to his footstool in prayer I may go,

And ask for a share in his love;

And if I thus earnestly seek him below,

I shall see him and hear him above. . . .

I long for the joy of that glorious time,

The sweetest, the brightest, the best;

When the dear little children of every clime

Shall crowd to His arms and be blest.

Prince of Peace

❧

PEACE I LEAVE WITH YOU,

MY PEACE I GIVE UNTO YOU:

NOT AS THE WORLD GIVETH,

GIVE I UNTO YOU. LET NOT

YOUR HEART BE TROUBLED,

NEITHER LET IT BE AFRAID.

—JOHN 14:27

As we ponder the impact of all the Savior has done, is doing, and will do for us, we can feel comforted, warmed, and filled. This is the power that emanates from the Son of God.

Here we see Christ in a courtyard scene, wearing a red robe, which identifies him as the Prince that he truly is. Several doves, which are the embodiment of peace, flock to him.

Even now, in our modern world of confusion and chaos, we can "be still and know that [he is] God" (D&C 101:16). We can trust in him as the true and constant source of peace, ever there if we will but let him in our hearts.

—Simon Dewey

GOSPEL PEACE

BRUCE R. MCCONKIE

Gospel peace! The peace possessed by the saints! What a marvelous blessing this is! "He who doeth the works of righteousness shall receive his reward, even peace in this world, and eternal life in the world to come." (D&C 59:23.) Christ is the Prince of Peace, the revealer and dispenser of that inner serenity known only to those who have received the gift of the Holy Ghost. Peace is one of the gifts of the Spirit. Thus, Jesus speaks not of the worldly salutation, "Peace be with you," which was commonly spoken among the Jews, but of that inner serenity reserved for those who have entered into the rest of the Lord and who know of the truth and divinity of the Lord's earthly kingdom.

(From The Mortal Messiah: From Bethlehem to Calvary, 4 vols. [Salt Lake City: Deseret Book, 1979–81], 4:78)

DROP THY STILL DEWS

JOHN GREENLEAF WHITTIER

Drop thy still dews of quietness till all our striving cease;

Take from our souls the strain and stress,

And let our ordered lives confess

The beauty of thy Peace.

"In the beginning was the Word, and the Word was with God, and the Word was God" (John 1:1).

It is no surprise that when the "Word was made flesh, and dwelt among us" (JST, John 1:14) that all nature would reverence the Creator to the extent that even the wind and the waves obeyed him.

We feel for the trembling apostles and acknowledge that when storms brew in the sea of life, we too become alarmed and perhaps forget that the Son of God once stood on the bow of a ship and, with his hand raised in power and authority, brought peace where there was tempest. That same Christ who has assumed his rightful place on high continues to have dominion over all creation. Our souls can be still knowing that even though we are minute in the immensity of all that is his, our Savior can calm the waves of trial and tribulation in each of our lives.

—Simon Dewey

Peace, Be Still

AND HE AROSE, AND REBUKED THE WIND,

AND SAID UNTO THE SEA, PEACE, BE STILL.

AND THE WIND CEASED, AND THERE

WAS A GREAT CALM.

—MARK 4:39

Simon Dewey

JESUS, LOVER OF MY SOUL

CHARLES WESLEY

Jesus, lover of my soul,

Let me to thy bosom fly,

While the nearer waters roll,

While the tempest still is high.

Hide me, O my Savior, hide,

Till the storm of life is past.

Safe into the haven guide;

Oh, receive my soul at last.

Other refuge have I none;

Hangs my helpless soul on thee.

Leave, oh, leave me not alone;

Still support and comfort me.

All my trust on thee is stayed;

All my help from thee I bring.

Cover my defenseless head

With the shadow of thy wing.

JESUS, SAVIOR, PILOT ME

EDWARD HOPPER

Jesus, Savior, pilot me

Over life's tempestuous sea;

Unknown waves before me roll,

Hiding rock and treach'rous shoal.

Chart and compass came from thee:

Jesus, Savior, pilot me.

As a mother stills her child,

Thou canst hush the ocean wild;

Boist'rous waves obey thy will

When thou say'st to them, "Be still!"

Wondrous Sov'reign of the sea,

Jesus, Savior, pilot me.

When at last I near the shore,

And the fearful breakers roar

'Twixt me and the peaceful rest,

Then, while leaning on thy breast,

May I hear thee say to me,

"Fear not: I will pilot thee."

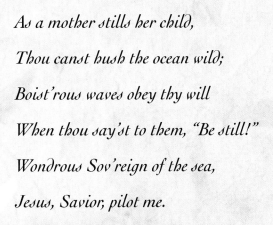

It is difficult to imagine the peace that must have come to those believers who walked in the presence of Jesus the Christ. Just being near the Master would have been remarkable, but then to have an ailment removed from the body—one that had plagued it for many years—would be a treasure of infinite worth.

Healing, for the most part, transpired after faith on the part of the afflicted combined with divine power from the Son of God to work a miracle. This same principle exists today. If we display faith sufficient, and if it is God's will, his power can work a mighty change within us, renewing us to perfect health. This is a true reminder that God is the same yesterday, today, and forever.

—Simon Dewey

Arise and Walk

✠

HEAL ME, O LORD, AND I SHALL BE HEALED; SAVE ME, AND I SHALL BE SAVED: FOR THOU ART MY PRAISE.

—JEREMIAH 17:14

Simon Dewey

Heal me, O Lord

THE SHEPHERD BOY'S SONG

JOHN BUNYAN

He that is down need fear no fall,

He that is low, no pride;

He that is humble, ever shall

Have God to be his guide.

I am content with what I have,

Little be it, or much:

And, Lord, contentment still I crave,

Because thou savest such.

Fulness to such, a burden is,

That go on pilgrimage;

Here little, and hereafter bliss,

Is best from age to age.

MIRACLES IN OUR DAY

SPENCER W. KIMBALL

A question often asked is: If miracles are a part of the gospel program, why do we not have such today?

The answer is a simple one: We do have miracles today—beyond imagination! If all the miracles of our own lifetime were recorded, it would take many library shelves to hold the books which would contain them.

What kinds of miracles do we have? All kinds—revelations, visions, tongues, healings, special guidance and direction, evil spirits cast out. Where are they recorded? In the records of the Church, in journals, in news and magazine articles and in the minds and memories of many people.

The rationalist continues: Many people are administered to and are not healed. That is true, as it has been in all times. It was never intended that all should be healed or that all should be raised from the dead, else the whole program of mortality and death and resurrection and exaltation would be frustrated.

However, the Lord does make specific promises: Signs will follow them that believe. He makes no promise that signs will create belief nor save nor exalt. Signs are the product of faith. They are born in the soil of unwavering sureness. They will be prevalent in the Church in about the same degree to which the people have true faith.

(From The Teachings of Spencer W. Kimball, *ed. Edward L. Kimball [Salt Lake City: Bookcraft, 1982], 499)*

The Lord Is My Shepherd

✤

I AM THE GOOD SHEPHERD,

AND KNOW MY SHEEP,

AND AM KNOWN OF MINE.

—JOHN 10:14

Simon Dewey

This painting tells a humbling story of the gift given and the gift received when a simple woman approached the Savior and proceeded to anoint his head with ointment, wash his feet with her tears, kiss them, and dry them with her hair. Perhaps she was caught up in mixed emotions—Godly sorrow for past indiscretions, coupled with the joy that can come only from the sweet cleansing words, "Thy sins are forgiven."

Indeed, it is our quiet acts of service, performed with love, that do a small part to repay our Savior for his ultimate gift. "Inasmuch as ye have done it unto one of the least of these my brethren, ye have done it unto me" (Matthew 25:40).

—Simon Dewey

For She Loved Much

HER SINS, WHICH ARE MANY, ARE

FORGIVEN; FOR SHE LOVED MUCH:

BUT TO WHOM LITTLE IS FORGIVEN,

THE SAME LOVETH LITTLE.

—LUKE 7:47

Simon Dewey

OTHERS

CHARLES D. MEIGS

Lord, let me live from day to day
  In such a self-forgetful way
That even when I kneel to pray,
  My prayers will be for others.

Help me in all the work I do
  To ever be sincere and true
And know that all I do for you
  Must needs be done for others.

Let "self" be crucified and slain
  And buried deep; and all in vain
May efforts be to rise again
  Unless to live for others.

And when my work on earth is done
  And my new work in heaven's begun,
May I forget the crown I've won
  While thinking still of others.

Others, Lord, yes, others,
  Let this my motto be;
Help me to live for others,
  That I may live like thee.

That I may live like thee

DROP, DROP, SLOW TEARS

PHINEAS FLETCHER

Drop, drop, slow tears,
 And bathe those beauteous feet
Which brought from heaven
 The news and prince of peace!
Cease not, wet eyes,
 His mercies to entreat;
To cry for vengeance
 Sin doth never cease;
In your deep floods
 Drown all my faults and fears;
Nor let his eye
 See sin but through my tears.

The impact of the Last Supper has reached across two millennia. And for Latter-day Saints, the sacrament is a weekly reminder of its symbolism and the Savior's subsequent sacrifice.

It was with deep symbolism that Christ took the bread, broke it, and offered it to his apostles; followed by the cup, which was also blessed and passed.

The sacrament is a vivid reminder that our Savior willingly allowed his body to be bruised and his lifeblood shed in order that we might live.

Perhaps the next time we take advantage of this wondrous gift, we will remember that there was a brief moment in history when a carpenter's hands took bread and broke it. And perhaps we will remember the other, excruciating moment in which those same hands were pierced with nails as the Savior paid a debt for us that we could not pay ourselves.

—Simon Dewey

The Last Supper

JESUS TOOK BREAD, AND BLESSED IT, AND BRAKE IT, AND GAVE IT TO THE DISCIPLES, AND SAID, TAKE, EAT; THIS IS MY BODY. AND HE TOOK THE CUP, AND GAVE THANKS, AND GAVE IT TO THEM, SAYING, DRINK YE ALL OF IT; FOR THIS IS MY BLOOD OF THE NEW TESTAMENT, WHICH IS SHED FOR MANY FOR THE REMISSION OF SINS.

—MATTHEW 26:26–28

Simon Dewey

HELP US, O GOD, TO REALIZE

AUTHOR UNKNOWN

Help us, O God, to realize

The great atoning sacrifice,

The gift of thy Beloved Son,

The Prince of Life, the Holy One.

THE SACRAMENT

DAVID O. MCKAY

———

Do we always stop to think, on that sacred Sabbath day when we meet together to partake of the sacrament, that we witness, promise, obligate ourselves, in the presence of one another, and in the presence of God, that we will do certain things? Note them.

The first: We are willing to take upon ourselves the name of the Son. In so doing we choose him as our leader and our ideal; and he is the one perfect character in all the world.

The second: That we will always remember him. Not just on Sunday, but on Monday, in our daily acts, in our self-control. When our brother hurts us, we are going to try to master our feelings and not retaliate in the same spirit of anger. . . . That's the spirit of the Christ, and that's what we have promised—that we will do our best to achieve these high standards of Christianity, true Christian principles.

The third: We promise to ". . . keep his commandments which he has given." . . . The obligation of a member of the Church of Jesus Christ is great, but it is as glorious as it is great, because obedience to these principles gives life, eternal life.

(From Gospel Ideals: Selections from the Discourses of David O. McKay *[Salt Lake City: Improvement Era, 1953], 146)*

The Bitter Cup

⁂

O MY FATHER, IF THIS CUP MAY

NOT PASS AWAY FROM ME, EXCEPT

I DRINK IT, THY WILL BE DONE.

—MATTHEW 26:42

Words fail when attempting to verbalize the enormity of the Atonement. While we cannot comprehend the Savior's feelings regarding his sacrifice, we can understand the facts surrounding it. We know that Christ inherited mortality from his mother, making his physical body susceptible to pain and anguish. And we know that as the Son of God, he volunteered to serve as a mediator for all people and thus endure suffering beyond what any mortal could bear.

Oh, the infinite wisdom of our Father in Heaven, to create this singular situation—with the knowledge that his beloved Son would be required to fulfill the plan in harrowing torment.

As we marvel at his love and sacrifice, let us do as the Savior instructed his apostles in Gethsemane, and pray that we enter not into temptation. And in that prayer, let us declare as the Savior did, in humble submission, "Not my will, but thine be done."

—Simon Dewey

'TIS MIDNIGHT; AND ON OLIVE'S BROW

WILLIAM B. TAPPAN

'Tis midnight; and on Olive's brow
  The star is dimmed that lately shone:
  'Tis midnight; in the garden now
The suffering Saviour prays alone.

'Tis midnight; and from all removed,
  The Saviour wrestles lone with fears;
  E'en that disciple whom He loved
Heeds not his Master's grief and tears.

'Tis midnight; and for others' guilt
  The Man of Sorrows weeps in blood;
  Yet He that hath in anguish knelt
Is not forsaken by His God.

'Tis midnight; and from heavenly plains
  Is borne the song that angels know;
  Unheard by mortals are the strains
That sweetly soothe the Saviour's woe. Amen.

GO TO DARK GETHSEMANE

JAMES MONTGOMERY

Go to dark Gethsemane,
Ye that feel the tempter's power;
Your Redeemer's conflict see;
Watch with Him one bitter hour;
Turn not from His griefs away;
Learn of Jesus Christ to pray.

See Him at the judgment hall,
Beaten, bound, reviled, arraigned;
See Him meekly bearing all;
Love to man His soul sustained;
Shun not suffering, shame or loss;
Learn of Christ to bear the cross.

Calvary's mournful mountain climb;
There adoring at His feet,
Mark that miracle of time,
God's own sacrifice complete:
"It is finished!" hear Him cry;
Learn of Jesus Christ to die. Amen.

Perhaps the most awesome event in history was that glorious moment when the Son of God stepped from the tomb and broke the chains of death that held us all bound. In that instant, majestic and triumphant, the singular act of sacrifice and love on the part of the Son and the Father bore fruit and gave us all the gift of life. As the sun rose upon that first Easter day, the world was never to be the same again. All things that had been created and were to be created would now live forever through this gift, unconditionally given. What sweet hope this gives us today, that we can all live again, and live eternally, if we will but submit our will to him who descended below all things that he might rise above all things.

"How sweet the joy this sentence gives, I know that my redeemer lives."

—Simon Dewey

He Lives

I AM THE RESURRECTION, AND THE

LIFE: HE THAT BELIEVETH IN ME,

THOUGH HE WERE DEAD, YET SHALL

HE LIVE: AND WHOSOEVER LIVETH

AND BELIEVETH IN ME SHALL NEVER DIE.

—JOHN 11:25–26

MY RISEN LORD

AUTHOR UNKNOWN

My risen Lord, I feel Thy strong protection;

I see Thee stand among the graves today;

"I am the Way, the Life, the Resurrection,"

I hear Thee say.

And all the burdens I have carried sadly

Grow light as blossoms on an April day;

My cross becomes a staff, I journey gladly

This Easter day.

CHRIST THE LORD IS RISEN TODAY

CHARLES WESLEY

Christ the Lord is ris'n today,

Sons of men and angels say, Alleluia!

Raise your joys and triumphs high,

Sing, ye heav'ns, and earth reply, Alleluia!

Love's redeeming work is done,

Fought the fight, the vict'ry won,

Jesus' agony is o'er,

Darkness veils the earth no more,

Lives again our glorious King,

Where, O Death, is now thy sting?

Once he died our souls to save,

Where thy victory, O grave?

Divine Redeemer

❧

ALL FLESH SHALL KNOW

THAT I THE LORD AM THY

SAVIOR AND THY REDEEMER,

THE MIGHTY ONE OF JACOB.

—ISAIAH 49:26

Simon Dewey

Index of Poems and Prose